THE INVISIBLE THRESHOLD

GW00480743

First published in 2012 by
The Dedalus Press
13 Moyclare Road
Baldoyle
Dublin 13
Ireland

www.dedaluspress.com

Copyright © Catherine Phil MacCarthy, 2012

ISBN 978 1 906614 60 7

All rights reserved.
No part of this publication may be reproduced in any form or by
any means without the prior permission of the publisher.

Dedalus Press titles are represented in the UK by
Central Books, 99 Wallis Road, London E9 5LN
and in North America by Syracuse University Press, Inc.,
621 Skytop Road, Suite 110, Syracuse, New York 13244.

Cover image: detail of *River and bank, The Quay,*
oil on canvas, 36 x 46 cm, 2010
Copyright © Bernadette Kiely

The Dedalus Press receives financial assistance from
The Arts Council / An Chomhairle Ealaíon

THE INVISIBLE THRESHOLD

Catherine Phil MacCarthy

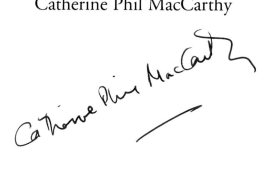

DEDALUS PRESS
DUBLIN, IRELAND

ACKNOWLEDGEMENTS

Acknowledgement is due to the editors of the following magazines and periodicals where some of these poems, or versions of them were first published: 'Limbo' won The Fish International Poetry Prize 2010, and was published in *The Fish Anthology 2010;* 'Turning South' was shortlisted for the Gregory O'Donoghue Poetry Prize 2010 and published in *Southword;* 'Turning South', 'Threshold', 'Facing the Rising Sun', 'Forecast', 'Rituals', 'Limbo', 'Capricorn', and 'Landlocked' were published in *New Hibernia Review.* Other poems are published in *Agenda, Poetry Ireland, The Stinging Fly, Southword, The Shop,* and *Salmon: A Journey in Poetry, Arena* on RTÉ Radio One, *Prairie Schooner,* and the Dedalus Press anthology *Shine On: Irish Writers for Shine.*

My thanks to The Arts Council of Ireland, An Comhairle Ealaíon, for a Bursary (multi-annual) in Literature in 2007/08 which enabled me to finish this collection. My gratitude, too, to Jonathan Williams, Literary Agent, for his guidance, to Jack Gilligan for the opportunity to work as Writer in Residence for Dublin City, and to Declan Kiberd for a Residency at the School of English, University College Dublin.

In memory of my sister, Betty
And in memory of my mother, Kathleen

CONTENTS

⤸

'The liminal – a word derived from the Latin for 'threshold' – is transitional. Every instant marks a liminal movement to the next thought and experience, a shift that may be smooth or turbulent, depending on how we choose to engage with it. It is also transformative; liminality stretches and relaxes, allowing new ideas, perspectives and understanding to be born.'

– John Hutchinson, *Saunter,* Douglas Hyde Gallery, Trinity College Dublin, 2009

'The imagination, like all things in time, is metamorphic. It is also rooted in a ground, a geography. The Latin word for the sacredness of a place is cultus, the dwelling of a god, the place where a rite is valid. Cultus becomes our word culture, not in the portentious sense it now has, but in a much humbler sense.'

—Guy Davenport, *The Geography of the Imagination*

Migrant

Will I see you one day soon, a beautiful man
I hardly know, walking, in the zone?

Will the nonchalant face of a lone figure
shine in the headlights one evening

as I slow down, stubble neat, hair
crew, long limbs aching for sleep?

Will I be stilled by vigour in the pace,
in the step something effortless and light?

Will you go from me as swiftly
as you came, into the world one stormy

September morning, hunger cries
causing milk in my breast to leak

and stream, rain after thunder
and lightning? Will you as freely return?

Sotto Voce

How clever the beech hedge –
still wearing a winter coat, leaves

crisp as onion skins, long into April.
It stands grappling with the breeze,

torn leaves scudding across cut grass –
amid plum and cherry blossom,

the white magnolia, formal as china –
as if it had outlived its season.

An old woman, oblivious of fashion
in a garden full of birdsong

whispers, who cares about time?
From my roots the sap extends,

buds hold tight as needles.
Come May, I'll yield to tender green.

Turning South

The road swerves and dips, slants south-east,
straight as a compass for miles between two ditches
alive with finches, fields of lambs and flowering gorse,
(sweet musk, pollen-breath of summer)

and straddling the end of that line on the horizon
as if it were designed, the Blackstairs,
a pyramid, only green, edging off the windscreen
as the road wound a slow descent

towards the river. That afternoon
as we strolled along, it was all sheer sunlit glitter
and fish jumping where we came to the din of a weir,
a lone heron stalked, keeled neck fully outstretched,

mimed such a motionless procession
that we stood there listening
to the rush of streams, happy water
weaving over stones, the endless chorus

of plain chant, a wordless uplift
as if time stopped and we were open to pure being,
indivisible from loved ones gone,
in the same place maybe, as the gates of heaven.

So when the breeze lifted sally leaves at the tree-tops,
in small bursts, inside the ancient woods
and let them drop, it sent a shiver,
as though they sensed the presence of God.

Taxi

Late for work he hails a taxi for the city,
lo and behold, now that he is driven all the way
and won't have to speed-walk from a late train down the quays,
he begins to breathe again, hear the driver rave, this morning's
    news,
a volcano in Iceland with an unpronounceable name
that has blown to high heaven so the plume of ash in the
    stratosphere
slowly drifts south-east into British air-space towards us,
do you credit that? No flights in or out today from anywhere.
Imagine, it could spew for years and we could all be stuck here.
No wonder they have free central heating and hot tubs everywhere
    you go
over there not to mention Katlya and did he hear how
locusts landing in a part of Australia as big as Spain yesterday
threatened to eat everything, ahead of the rain? That's when they
    breed,
moth-like in size and clustered deep.

Heatwave

Lots more fish, her mother said.
She could see only the one,

down past the tennis courts in summer
striding along the river,

books in his hand,
looking straight ahead,

bushman's hat,
great black coat trailing him.

When he turned to her in June
their tongues pressed
innocent and hard against teeth,
then soft and lingering.

The blue of a dress on the grass,
the heat of her skin.

Beside them, pale leaves
of the weeping willow hung

in the water and speckled trout
in the current swam upstream.

Lost Shoe

When she woke the morning after,
hardly the worse for wear,
she could find only one silver slipper –
(though she looked everywhere)

one, of a favourite pair, lost
in The Palace the night before
in a dash to the cloakroom,
leaving the dance floor.

No way would she phone
lost property, or speak to a doorman.
This girl would take the measure
of Prince Charming.

Orchard

Under the floorboards when we first moved in
to M A N O A H, white enamel letters
on the glass above the door, we spotted
three foot below on foundation clay

the dun and blue wave-pattern notebook
disclosed pages of translucent sepia,
numbered, ruled and dated,
an inventory of garden produce:
red currants, peaches, Victoria plums,
tomatoes, and lettuce, sold in pound boxes
by the dozen to Alex Findlater & Co,
Fletchers of Smithfield or W.H. Cole.

The stylish handwriting of H.F. Poole
flowing from July 1930 to March '33
detailed a universe
that had not yet seen the night of
the long knives or Kristallnacht,

while before us on that sunny afternoon –
the slow ravages of time,
gnarled stumps of apple and pear,
an orchard overgrown with brambles,
honeysuckle, a butterflies' paradise,
ready to be reclaimed and re-sown,
shells of greenhouses strewn with terracotta,
and glass shards sunk in loamy earth
unseen, that would turn up for years.

Desert Island

They must have been caught in a rip?
One minute up to the waist, then to the neck,
the huge swell hauled the fearless girl in a channel

screaming for help, the boy yelled against the current.
Cook swam, lifted the youngest above the waves
and trod the rising undertow. The boy was beyond reach,

out of depth, dog paddling back, frantic limbs losing ground
every second, hair standing on end. *HELP!*
went unheard amid all the excitement,

in a foreign language. All she could do was hope.
When water lost its grip, they were washed up,
miles from home, castaways, on a sandy shore.

Threshold

Father and son tidied up the yard,
made all about the house clean,
mowed the lawn. All the young
men in the family joined in,
prepared the place – in that way –
for her going, called rake
and wheelbarrow into commission,
the afternoon acrid with a scent
of diesel and cut grass.
They worked late and came in
that evening, like men long ago
home from the meadow,
an air about them of appetite
and completion, so preparations
would be echoed in heaven –
here, a wife and mother leaving,
there, a daughter welcome.

September Equinox

i.

The overcast sky threatens rain.
Where has our longed-for summer
gone? All along the pavement fuchsia
blossom, carmine pools – these bright falls
harbinger of a world you are absent in.

ii.

Your face to one side so white
on the pillow. A candle is lit.
Breath so slight,
is it sleep or death?

iii.

A grave lined with leaves of laurel
and rose. White, red and orange blooms,
threaded down walls, layer the floor:
scents of a summer garden await the coffin.

Skojcan Journey

Across the bleached stepping stones,
river down to a soundless trickle, lazy pools
lukewarm in the shade, we speak of the rains
that flooded the canyon last summer,
trace the high water-mark by driftwood
sticks high above our heads, a tangle
in branches of a linden like the nest
of some great bird – eagle, or peregrine falcon
we've seen riding the thermals in pairs
above the cliffs, four, skyward, circling
into azure further than the eye could see,
or maybe a crane, last glimpsed with fox
in the fresco of a tiny church. Black,
the magnesium line stains limestone walls
way up so that even now a tumult rages
and we are treading the Reka river-bed,
hands loosening our boots while we float
free, water-sprites in the chasm of a deep rush,
our hair standing on end, amidst a melee
of drowned debris, branches of morello
and plum, berries of wild fruit, stalks
of flowering cyclamen, lizard, snake
and wolf, all swept past the broken mill-
wheel, through the gorge mouth, down and down
through timeless caves, where only this
river flows, coursing into the underworld.

The Bat

Church doors wide open,
the bat came flying in
that October evening,

dark wings splayed,
swooped over the congregation
in packed pews,

across the silent altar,
stirring the air above
the celebrant,

drew a ripple from children
gathered for Communion,
levitated for their eyes.

Flew high as the rafters,
creature of night skies,
tiny claws quivered past

solemn readings from Isaiah,
the Gospel of St Mark?
Chose this occasion

to run amok,
to turn the heads of girls
in best dresses,

small boys in long pants,
break all the rules,
eerily, to dance?

Facing the Rising Sun

After your death in the small hours –
the sun came up, clouds rent and parted,
all the night-lying fog dispersed,
so light drenched fields and trees

shimmered with a rainy greenness,
the incessant song of small birds
and shifting cobalt veils crosslit the sky,
a sense of first breath on the earth, of birth.

The Way We Work

What lies hidden
this November morning of squally rain
at dawn and fallen leaves

is your body lonely
under earth in that small hilly graveyard
sheltered by yews,

is your flesh free
of disease, disintegration complete,
wrists at last shell-clean

down to the skeleton
you first came across at school,
Latin on your tongue a song,

fibula, patella, talus, all the bones
you knew the names of
learnt as a nurse,

knowledge, beyond
words, of what
connects us.

Forecast

'… a future forbidden to no one.'
— Derek Mahon

This afternoon I wish you were still here
to see from our study window

how the dark lavender maelstrom of cloud
loading the skies over Dublin

is shot with light, so that whatever
appeared threatening in it an hour ago –

widespread flash floods across the city
even hailstones – has settled into

something less than weather and more
shy of attention, a painter's slate

lit with burnt umber and old rose,
densities lifted and electrified now

across the whole dimension of air
with untold possibilties.

Young Wife

Cows emerge one by one in dawn fog –
dewy coats of colour: short-horn, friesian, roan –
as if their materiality is contingent on her presence
and the early morning scene in Loughlin's field

below the turn, some after-life from a painting
titled *Woman and Cows in Heaven*,
while she stands there scanning the white drift –
senses cold from the ground through her feet,

the thin fabric of her dress, under a cross-over apron –
covets the life ahead, as the world about her sleeps,
this freedom of standing alone on a farm of their own
before milking, woman of the house, taking stock.

Móin na nGé

The signpost in Irish made sense –
my mother's pronunciation
all those years of Monagea –
put me in mind of Camas
one evening just saying good-bye,
a gaggle of slow geese

bustling across the road-field
to the pond by the gate
in a straggling line, imperious,
serene, ladies in white-flounced lace
in late summer heat ambling to a ball,
ready at the least inspection

to take umbrage, lift wings
and flap, rush long snake-like necks
across the stand at us and hiss,
flightless birds, poised
for ambush or take off,
glean in advance –

nothing to do with a golden egg,
more: precious goose fat,
strongest quills pared
for a pen, downy feathers
plucked for a quilt, beside the range,
that sinewy span, a goose-wing.

* *Móin na nGé,* goose marsh

Fires

My mother's dying is like a fire
burning low,
a restless tongue of blue that flares up suddenly
in a darkening room,

a brilliant glow that
consumes the last embers whole,
throws our unearthly shadows on the ceiling,
blazes and sparks,

threatens never to leave us,
like the fires of old
she banked with coal. How she coaxed
the flaming logs, ash or oak,

with a thin crust of slack
that smoked and spat, slowed things down
and soon turned molten,
in the same breath lamented

the feast of the Holy Souls,
swearing to keep winter from the door.

Harry Houdini

'My purpose is to tell of bodies that have been
transformed into shapes of a different kind.'
　　—Ovid, *Metamorphoses*

Tied in a sack and locked in a trunk,
he was able to switch on stage with his wife.
So this is what? To slip the lock of words,
and throw the bolt, move at the speed of sound?

Any wonder I'm scared. Unable to utter a word.
Mister Metamorphoses, named 'eehrie'
by his friends. Extricated himself from
fishing nets, milk churns, steam pots locked with

rivets, and once the belly of a whale.
His bones were soft, my father suggested,
malleable as rubber. As if this explained
those challenge acts and water torture cells.

Rituals

Most nights he lifted the latch of the hall door
paced out the yard in the dark
gingerly stepping the uneven patch
where a shrub rose bloomed late

on the whitewashed wall between two gates,
the sky livid with stars,
to enter the neighbours' place,
sit down and discuss the world by the warm stove.

My mother crocheted by the hot range.
When he came back in, we would be called
to bend our knees and say 'a few decades',
discover our father

lowered from reading the paper.
At the end, she recited the *Hail Holy Queen*,
all the while her eloquence growing

with the *Litany of the Blessed Virgin*,
words flowing on, too mysterious to decipher,
Seat of wisdom, Cause of our joy, House of gold.

Elbows planted on painted green of the chairs,
five of us gathered around her chorused *Pray for us*,
shifted from one knee to the other
on the flagstone floor.

Limbo

The firstborn   was handed back to them
in a small cask   not much bigger than
a shoebox   only wooden   no more about it
they took it home by pony and trap
wasn't the river in flood at the gate?
they had to climb down   and wade through it
and she went alone with him
to the corner of a field   below the house
a dry shaded place   where he opened a grave
for it was April then   and the pinkish
blossoms of whitethorn were emerging
and they lifted it low together
onto sods of damp earth
placed holy water with it
and everything she could to lay
a holy innocent to rest
as far as giving the boy   a name
it was Martin   the brother in Chicago
and when it came to saying good-bye
he had to draw her away   she was so
lonely   that shook him   while
he covered it with clay   for up to then
never a care   but a demon for style
high heels   you've never seen the like
though she gave birth again
she was often seen   alone   in that field

Television News

A sleeping babe in swaddling clothes
is cradled from hand to hand
by men in a long line,
dressed in ivory kurtas.
Knee-deep in monsoon floods,
they deliver an infant from
treacherous mud-water, as if
mother was the ancient river.

Maternity

I. ULTRASOUND

She views his infant length   anchored
in amniotic peace   that foetal curve
all the way from   slightly bowed head
hands crossed at the chest   a solemn promise
fingers ten   bewildered baby face
seen for the first time   alone   ruminating
not yet seeing   down to the wrinkled soles of feet
her laughter relief   not used to   seeing her insides
on screen   a satellite image   of world weather

all routine   the doctor says   he can't detect
a second heartbeat   sudden alert
he takes all the time in the world   to place
cold gel again to her round abdomen
Isn't one enough for everyone?
the answer then   *it picks up yours first*

for the longest while   she holds still
takes in the sight of her baby   gives time
to find   as if this is a game of hide and seek
she counts   all the way to twenty-five
hands over eyes   then soundlessly turns
and calls   *ready or not, here I am*
they stare   at the screen   unmoved
eyes on the cursor   slowly travelling
a bright arrow   adrift   a tiny vessel
on a wild ocean   *see* he sighs   *nothing*

for a moment   they peer together
like boy and girl   searching   for a pinhead star
that comes and goes in grey drizzle   and then another
close needle of rain   hitting dark sea
pulsing   her love child   twenty-two weeks

would you like a glass of water?
she finds on the chair   a crumpled heap
draws her pink dress   over her head
of course there was the spotting
in the ladies   at midday   start of rehearsal
but hardly enough to warrant
when he returns   moves a chair close
the hardest news   you'll ever hear
need all your courage   to bear
before he has time to say   more
but how can you be sure?   slips from her throat
how can a mere machine know?
it would appear   the heart has stopped
the words are uttered without fear
she shrugs as if found wanting   for the first time
a twinge of recognition   admits a blind tear
he persists   *it happens   one in four*
nature's way   not usually this late
we can't be sure exactly why

II. DELIVERY ROOM

Louder now   from somewhere   down the corridor
two women   lumber past the door
heavily laden bodies speak of 'full-term'
and 'overdue'   they talk of how to   bring on the birth
mother casually   by the window   light up
hope intact   she sees them from another world
sentenced for the moment to   doing time

urgent   in the background   a scream
from the floor above   trials of someone
in labour   where a nurse holds a hand
urges   push   push   with all your might
she was there   before   with her first
senses sweat   break   in a cold film
how her laden body   extended then
discovering   animal grace   in primal rhythm
pain   released in a paroxysm
now the spasm   lifted her spine

she dug in her heels
she could feel   the head   slowly jamb
down through the birth canal
intent   and unstoppable   knowing its own   destiny
her hips danced   and his arms
held her shoulders in traction
her pelvis   threatened to split open
as the waves   coursed through her and carried
and carried   way beyond the riverbed   of herself to the tidal
stream   that deep channel   pulsing to the ocean

her ripe fullness   doomed   to its own pleasure   of coming
and coming   on a high wire   of bringing
their child into the world
where a baby's distinct cries
are heard loud in the labour ward

III. Night

She sees this baby   in her mind's eye
black and white   photos of an infant
the boy next door   when she was a child
blond   fine-boned   sturdy   ever-present
side by side in darkness
                              they hold hands
sound asleep   she dreams   the wide ocean
flying beneath   as twin-engines stall
suddenly   in mid-air   the cabin
sucked clean of oxygen   a door flung
open   her lungs yawn   in slow motion
against the vacuum
                              blood seeps from
her womb   over the sheets   a flood-plain
contractions deepen   pain leaps to sear
a fine needle   penetrates   her spine
the anaesthetist   pledges to be there
when she wakes   she is wheeled into
theatre   has no memory   of labour
of suture   though the face above her
blurs and fades   continues to gaze
through the black
                              thick rims of his glasses
words drift singly from his lips   petals
in cotton-wool ether of the room
don't   worry   now   love   sleep

Time Out of Mind

He might as well have landed on the moon.
From blue bewildered eyes his ice-cold
stare scuttles each attempt to reassure.
Have I been here before, he wonders

eyeing the window, the wardrobe, the chair,
craters all, in the nursing home as if for
the first time. No memory of where
he's spent the last year, of who his offspring

are. *Did I walk through my own door?*
he hazards tentatively, neither here
nor there, weightless as an astronaut
suspended on a starless lunar night.

Irish Elk

Giant antlers shine at night
diamond, sapphire, branch

in a neighbour's garden, light
up the moonless dark

for children going to bed,
as if the Great Irish Elk,

extinct seven thousand years,
turned in his grave

beneath the lake at Lough Gur,
and bellowing rose

from the bog, trailing peat
from his hinds, to roam

the hills and woods of Ireland,
at this time of snow

falling all across the land,
on our road, ghost at

large, and twice as tall as Man
come back to haunt us.

Winter Solstice

The low-lit branches of the lilac,
startling as skin this morning,
only place in the garden
the sun's reflection,
like your absence
concentrates.

Capricorn

A week before Christmas we fled
the city's labyrinth,
traffic jams, tailbacks, endless
lights en route to the airport

for a village in the high Alps
where the sky burned with stars
and in the morning snowfields
opened out above the pines,

decorated with discrete tracks
that vanished in unfettered whiteness,
as if the creature became air,
marmot, rabbit, ibex, deer.

US Airways Flight 1549

Those gazing out of mid-town windows
saw what they'd never seen,
a jet land clean on water,
some magnificent bird's skate
entirely lost in spray,
and, seconds later, one rare

sea creature, too big for river,
an exotic whale come up for air like Jonah's,
some leviathan of the atmosphere
disgorging onto wings,
drifting downstream in January
an orderly line of people standing.

The House, Thoor Ballylee

'And what if my descendants lose the flower
Through natural declension of the soul ... ?'
　　—W. B Yeats, *Meditations in Time of Civil War, IV*

What might you have foreseen? The way that rain
teemed all autumn on the ragged elm
so fields were flooded and the river rose
on your precious acre of stony ground?

How water crept round the ancient tower,
and swept old trees in the eyes of the bridge,
immersed the road, welled up the winding stair
so that each intake of breath was a magnet

for a river in spate and the torrent flowing in
the chamber window met waters flowing out?
That table, of trestles and board where you wrote,
a fire of turf in the open grey hearth:

*and know whatever flourish and decline
these stones remain their monument and mine.*

March in the Alps

We arrived the morning the weather settled,
after months of freezing fog and blizzards
like waking to a clear spring day in Ireland,
an air of something indefinable –

a sun that warmed, and no wind, the world
already turned, though snowbound mountains
dazzled and beckoned and icicles glistened

in the valley, songbirds echoed, the earth
relaxed before inevitable thaw, deep down
the whole panorama minted new.

Suddenly

The life and soul of the party,
so bright and warm and urbane –
extolled us on plans for the New Year

last time we met. It could have been
a stroke, though tall and gangly he was,
seeing him slump over the wheel

on his way home from work,
the car veering off the road onto a pavement
before it teetered to a standstill

and in the silent afternoon an ambulance
siren echoed – it was after all how
uncle at fifty-two years was struck.

It might have been a heart attack
or a clot moving to the brain.
Maybe a head-on collision in the small hours

as recounted in the daily papers?
Sex or drugs, instant collapse?
Much darker than you think, his friend

interposed. I felt my own breath
retract. No pictures came. Nothing I could bear
to imagine. Shrugging off

the numbing mantle –

Convention

The snowbound cricket pitch
is flocked with Brent Geese
this arctic January morning,
massed gabbling heads,
a black throng of consternation –

Emperor

He charmed the birds
in his silk suits, spent years
brokering deals overseas.
Apartments. Market-shares.
When they recognized the shift
in his style, face covered for
the camera, they failed to realise
that he had pinched our gold,
traded the lives of our children.
We are still meant to sign
despite all, *their* conditions?
Eat thin gruel? Apply for a loan?
Listen to the boy's loud cry.
Live in an unjust realm?
Might as well take to the streets.
What people have always done:
Swallow the royal yarn,
join the queues for the dole.

Working Women at TK Maxx

Ralph Lauren, DKNY, Calvin Klein.
How much I'd lost my way to be

wandering the aisles at lunch-break,
unsure which direction to take,

racks of high-street brands for miles,
women's and men's, left and right

amid countless stands of handbags,
négligés, no window in sight.

She swept past like a cold current
in the sea over the whole body,

eyes lowered to the bargain in my hand,
its logo of two bones crossed,

Billabong, M, marl, men's underwear.
Her presence enlivened me

to ask who are we, our silence
saying we are only real elsewhere,

no longer human in this place
of stale air and artificial light,

no less superfluous than clothes
remaindered, and selling at half-price.

Overseas Mission

'Noblest of men, woo't die?
Hast thou no care of me?'
    —William Shakespeare, *Cleopatra*

I. THE FIRST PEACEKEEPERS 1958

That June it meant escaping the dull grind
of Border duty, military drill,
a household of caterwauling children.
They hardly knew where they were going

as they stood under the aeroplane's wing
waving, in worsted moss-green uniforms,
bulls' wool overcoats draped over arms,
bound for the first overseas mission

to the Lebanon. Everything they trained for –
observation posts, scouts for smugglers
on the Syrian frontier. Those who came back
to the wife long pregnant, new baby,

the family farm, united in kinship,
talked of relations between Cairo
and Jerusalem, on their map,
Suez, the Gaza strip, Mount Sinai.

II. After the Congo

They brought him home by ship –
Matadi to Antwerp – all those latitudes,
casket draped in the tricolour, and blue
U.N. flag, then the *City of Waterford* to Cork

and Dublin. Two officers accompanied
his coffin. On the long funeral procession,
passers-by knelt on the wet pavements
from Arbour Hill to Glasnevin.

He was given a hero's welome,
laid to rest with full military attention.
They brought him home from the equator,
buried him in an Irish winter;

after river, ocean, shifts in temperature,
at the grave, his wife and son, weeping.

III. Soldier

Driven from the heat of the kitchen
you lay on the grass under a flowering apple –

where grew in spring snowdrop and cyclamen
as mother had carefully planted them –

mossy lawn in June easy as a cushion,
explored blue infinity through apple blossom,
inhaled the warm aromatic drift along with roses,
found that nothing could dispel the silence,

a certain vacancy, how the whole house,
a monument to whose memory – photos, *objets,*
bedroom – was still waiting for his return,

laden with the pressure of things unspoken
between them, everything he'd flown away from

and never laid eyes on again
down to the joint roasting in the oven –

Making *Fitzcarraldo*

... to prove the inner chronicle of who we are
—Werner Herzog

The white hull juts between trees
in the rainforest, half-way up a mountain,
a three-story steamer, on a steep incline.
When the camera moves closer,
we see it winched on pulleys,
creaking upwards through sludge,
inch, by slow inch, to the plateau of an isthmus,
high piercing cries of tropical birds
where sky is the only limit.
A haul-line snaps, the capstan rolls
back amid bedlam from the locals,

drawing a myth up such an unlikely 'river' –
Enrico Caruso in an Opera house in Iquitos?
Young stage-hands, faces painted,
stripped to the waist, lithe bodies
put to the test, husbands, brothers, sons,
minute against the bow, stall
the colossal weight against gravity,
yellow snakes, warring tribes, jungle isolation
while the ship takes down a man,
before the eyes of his friends,
no time to jump clear –

Coolacrease: Looking Back

'The land was ours before we were the land's.'
— Robert Frost, 'The Gift Outright'

No one saw it come. Out of the blue. A rifle shot.
We were startled by the clamour. My mother slept on.
A distant thud from the road. The echo of an axe.
Then the crash as the tree split and men's voices argued

as if it was daylight. How dare they? At midnight.
The boys went down. Fired a shot to frighten them.
Next day cleared the road-block. Up at all hours,
alone in the meadow, a week later they turned hay.

In the big field behind the house. Sun.
splitting the stones. Father and my youngest brother
went to town. Pen knives and a new edging stone,
baling twine? New blades for the scythes.

A meeting miles away that morning?
The boys were leaning on their forks when they saw
men in a line, crest the hill, spread wide.
The flying column? One who was our postman shouted,

Run! They stood their ground. Why would they run?
The wild cry was a cock pheasant lifting from grass
disturbed by all the fuss. Shouts from the headland –
I stood with hands covered in flour and stared

from the back door, as if I was Lot's wife.
Fear rose from the ground. The breeze cooled
the sweat on my brow as I counted armed men
in a line. Thirty of them? *We are under orders,*

one called, *You are planter people, guilty of treason,*
in league with the crown. What was that about?
Some trouble over the Mass path. Locals
held a passage through it. Though friends

no longer spoke. My father, a traitor? Running
messages for the RIC? What was there to hide?
We read the bible in the evenings. Went to a Catholic school.
The boys played hurling for the local team. My sister

liked Irish dancing. Walked out with an English officer.
The raiders marched into the kitchen where we were baking.
My mother must have fainted and was carried into the grove
where we followed after. I asked a raider *Why?*

You could have kept your heads down. He was masked
and backed away slowly. I looked into his eyes. Fear.
Of being recognised? If only father arrived home then.
Did he know something? The volley from the courtyard –

the men were shouting and running all over.
Someone cycled off to find a doctor. I found my two
brothers slumped by the wall. The house was burning.
A stink of petrol everywhere. We dragged

a mattress out, and laid the boys side by side.
By the time the doctor came, they were losing.
After the burial, the ruins still smouldered.
We lived in the coach-house. Amid roses

in bloom, the fragrance of wild woodbine.
Laburnum, oak, ash, pine. The land was ours,
and we were now its people. Emigrating to Australia.
I was Irish in Victoria.

Daughter of the House

The headlights of the car
that dropped him late in the yard,
lit branches of the ash
splayed across the sky as it slipped
down the lane. Black patch

over one eye like an old captain
he stooped at the door,
pitch of the night on his shoulders,
cleared rheum from his throat and spat,
then made his entrance – mother
already winding the clock for dawn.

The crutch pushed to one side,
he sank into a wooden armchair.
From the safety of father's arms,
stricken, she eyed the intruder past winks,
jokes, mock grimaces,
as if he found in her eyes

fault with his own reflection,
her face unable to hide
through the dumb show of *peepo*
what the adults couldn't bear to show him:
the colossal wreck of his body,
clay pipe in his hand still smoking.

The game, a tired distraction,
gave way to that ear-to-the-ground,
soon to be well-oiled divagation
on land-prices or cattle,
the cost of buying in hay
or animal bedding, the flooded meadow.

It taught something of friendship
and something of sorrow, an old seer,
bred on hardship and marrow, betting on
that winning greyhound of a country.

As a parting shot he opened
his pocket watch, engraved silver frame
on its intricate touch-me-not face as
the second hand slid tick-stop-tick-stop-tick
in even beats like her heart,
his one eye, a tawny eagle's,
seemed to say —

damn it all for a story
I am still the man I used to be.

Father & Son

He beat Sonny once, the way
O'Leary chastised him,
a customary flogging with the leather strap,
Mind, I'll tan his hide, or *I'll wallop*
the living daylights out of him,
said with pride, with talk of how
urgent it was to *make a man of him.*
Back then we heard rumours, how
granny scolded for giving 'her boy'
the stick, questioned the right to harm
a hair on his head, least of all a first-born.
All forgotten, until days later, after school,
as he swam in the river, bruises were jeered,
black and purple turning to yellow mapped
the pale skin of a slender buttock.
A thing of nothing, his nonchalance
greeted our perplexed shock, the whole
misfortune troubled us no less than
the Old Testament, Isaac and Abraham.

Exiles

'...and thou shalt smite the rock,
and there shall come water out of it.'
—Exodus 17:6

At your table I read in the Torah
how the Israelites set down camp,
after weeks of wandering in the desert,
no place of seeds, or figs, grapevines

or pomegranates. Before the elders,
Moses struck water from rock,
more than a damp seep on the face of stone.
A channel, issuing a small stream,

deepened to gorge spilling down a river
to flood the valley and bathe their flock.
Lost tributary of the Jordan,
poetry of the dreamtime, faithful

map of how poems spring like answered
prayers, against all odds, to slake thirst
after cursing Moses, blaming God
and going out to a foreign land.

Writer's Block

Have you lost your tongue?
This, in front of visitors in the parlour
when called on to perform.
The polished mahogany table
was covered in white linen.
On the sideboard, whiskey,
lemonade, cigarettes, port wine.
My confidence waned
and where was my song?
Now many years on, the meaning
comes back to me again,
blank page facing me down,
the request so irredeemable,
Where have you been and why
have you not been practising?

Black Magic

All I recall now of us two
together, ever, is that moment

I pointed up to hatboxes
in the half-light of the big room

with windows north and south.
Not how we came to conspire

or how, at ninety-two, you balanced
on a chair to hand down that gift

the size of a treasure chest,
bound with red ribbon and left

by visitors the days before.
None of that came home to roost,

only that I was chancing my arm
and not able to speak yet

when I pointed in the gloom
looking for your attention.

You stared uncomprehending
and I kept on blundering

as you leaned down to hear
my first syllables.

Landlocked

Dust thou art and into dust.
Words of the sermon on Sunday morning

in a world that knew nothing of cocaine.
This was mud on Sunday afternoon banked

by the fresh-water pool at Ringmoylan,
our first swimming lessons in the open air,

chill water creeping to the waist, murky, green
smelt of the loamy river instead of the sea.

Rough-cast walls and floor inimical
to four-year-old feet. Children paddled

or clung to concrete edges, stared at
a shoreline of wet mounds, gleaming

in the sun like melted chocolate,
seeming to breathe tiny rivulets.

A psychedelic dream? Silt at low tide,
the underbelly of the Shannon exposed like

a shame, complete in its own isolation.
Where was the thundering sea that looked

towards America, clear water lapping
at our heels, sand fine-grained, pristine?

Ballybunion, Salthill, Kilkee?
Why were we here? This silent riverbed

led nowhere like some forgotten reverie,
due soon to disappear, a tidal swamp

divulging random debris, the wheelless
frame of a bicycle, a rusty axle ridged deep,

some doll's pram, upturned, the shallow
backwater threatening to steal.

Tying the Knot

after Brancusi

I must have been on the cusp
seeing my first couple kiss.
A soap on TV? Curious
I imagined them

undressed and bound
so close with string
or cord or swaddling band,
flesh so deeply magnetised

they became one
and in that state of betrothal
would no more separate again
than Eve and Adam.

Next to contemplate how
they could eat or drink
since no space was left
between their lips.

They no longer hunger
or thirst for anything
but skin and bone become
one. From week to week

I stole glimpses at the screen
with no iota of who my own
sweetheart might be or where
on earth to go looking.

Shining Armour

His hair was longer then, she said, what's more
I could only agree, thinking of jet
Che Guevara locks and beard, the combat
jacket and denim jeans almost threadbare

at the knee when he knelt to mend the gears
of my bike and I could see skin so white
and worthy of an Italian sonnet,
I nearly reached out to touch it where

he sat cross-legged on the floor
drinking beer all strong limbs and ease,
snug at his hip money and keys
on a belt from Spain or Greece,

an air of being on his way somewhere,
in his pocket the secret of changing the planet.

Drift

I was standing at the waterline,
looking out to sea, on the rim of a new day,
the last, of a holiday.

We had not yet spoken when he placed
in my palm, this older man grown filial,
a young sea urchin's shell.

We said not a word but the green of his irises
round the dark pupil enveloped mine,
then that intricate design.

Fragile completion waited for my reaction,
that morning of my son living away from home
for the first time.

Forest Walk at Glendalough

High up among the pines
at Glendalough, above the falls
at Coolnabass, past hazel, willow
and birch, past oak, yew, and larch,

there's no one to be seen.
Voices echo from the ridge,
or from somewhere below
in the valley, dappled laughter.

Rabbits nibble the sunny verge,
stilled by the beat of our footfall.
As we halt, young deer grazing
on sphagnum along the edge

turn heads and gaze with eyes
of liquid wonder. In seconds they lift
long forelegs and vanish
into deep darkness of the forest.

Time and again their curiosity
gives way – once they sense
we are human and share
the same earth – to dread.

Anniversary

You died before the news broke –
the failure of large, American banks,

Lehman Brothers, Merrill Lynch.
It was all going on, in the networks

that week, as morphine levels increased
in your veins, the neighbours called in,

and your family took turns by your bed.
Now it would be difficult to explain

exactly what was meant when *'western
civilisation, as we know it'* began to upend,

the night Nancy Pelosi called up the Fed,
prayers ran in and out of your mouth like

birds and you came to draw your last breath.
Little did any of us know how images

of Wall Street like a ghost town emerged,
or how you would eclipse the woes of

Fannie Mae and Freddie Mac, names
that might easily crop up

around Knockea in neighbourly gossip.
So much for all that wealth. Words like

sub-prime, toxic, and lethal, attempt to
redress. *Anglo* and NAMA persist like

bad spells. If you were to come back,
all we could say is the planet has changed.

Rain the whole summer long before
your death seems a portent.

How we manage in your absence?
Will our children create a different world?

Are we better off, packing our bags,
preparing for the next?

Night Sky

Paint at night those
stars in a frosty sky,
one brighter than another,

Sirius, Orion, Great Bear.
Accustom eyes to deepest pitch
that delivers the Milky Way.

The more it's scanned,
this sprawl grows fathomless.
Too late to catch low in the south –

as if the sound made
walking the lane just now
frightened it away –

a star falling and seconds later
another, lit trajectory
scorching headlong

over the western rim.
Yet, up above the heavens are
crammed with constellations like

so many freckles jostling for place.
Could it be some night
we are not there,

gone without trace,
planet earth, an empty house
as the face of night prevails,

unforeseen and certain
from the beginning
as only death is?

Sauntering to Ourense

'Some, however, would derive the word form *sans terre*, without land or a home, which, therefore, in the good sense, will mean, having no particular home, but equally at home everywhere.'
—H.D. Thoreau, *Walking*, 1862

The sky was that wan blue before dawn.
A faint star or two dallied as we trailed

in pairs and threes. Flocks of swallows
lifted in the breeze along the river,

excited by our voices, scattered overhead;
that noiseless chorus of wing-beats,

herald to our journey, alerted us, if call
was necessary, to air light as champagne,

rinsed by night-rains across the Roman bridge
of Rio Miño, to our less travelled road,

mapped and worn for centuries, become
second nature and all, still ahead of us, and summer.

When the Dust Settles

On Lansdowne Road, right by the new stadium
cherry trees still bloom. The monumental tiffany dome
refracts the heat of the sun, broods
over a street of Victorian redbricks

where old gardens flourish. Mature trees
defy wonders of the boom, promise irretrievable Dublin.
As if this were a first spring, damson, malus, plum,
pink heads reach past the builders' veneer.

Dream Music

The boat is pushed out,
the rudder-cord cleated in tight,
dagger board's down, my feet stretch against
the far deck as I shift the rudder away,
the sail swings out, slapping loud
this light vessel bobs about, finds wind
the prow bucks like a runaway horse, picks up speed,
the sheet is a tangled web at my bare feet
all business, one hand gathers and loops, the other spills wind
to gauge the tension against the huge pull as the sail balloons
strong and full, its hang on for dear life,

and I'm stretched over the side my back against the spray,
this long hull digs low as if it were a plough slicing through brine,
wake-music builds in my ears, it's a hollowed-out canoe from
aeons ago when the road was the sea,
a Brendan currach,
a Levantine galley,
a fallukah with a mind of its own
that carries me,

always the prospect imminent of a gust
that hauls the rope from my hands and overturns the keel,
or a sudden drop and the sail brings the mast crashing on top
        of me
and all hell but I've learnt to stay on,
use the wind to cut through the swell,
skirt hidden rocks, the doldrums, dead man, no go zones,
to draw the rope so tight, the boat hums and sings as it flies
through the waves, making the deep bow-string notes
of viola, or cello, soon the whole quartet
as bird and bee even a yellow butterfly are greeted out here,

and my eyes take in the line of the coast,
breeze riffs on water,
honey-combs of light on the sandy floor,
starfish, black sea-slugs like great hairy mollies,
the frenzy of herring shoals,
how far to go, rise and fall into deep troughs,
before I slacken pace ready to tack,
push the rudder out wide, swing around fast,
map horizon points to hold course, towards steeple
or mountain peak, across the wide bay, on a run to the shore.

Storm

The tree is shaking its head at the wind
and throwing up empty hands in fury
and the wind, the wind is running away,
legs gathering speed, running
across the far fields to the sea.

Lightning Source UK Ltd.
Milton Keynes UK
UKOW050207040712

195428UK00001B/27/P